DISCOVER THROUGH CRAFT

THE
MAYA

Jillian Powell

W
FRANKLIN WATTS
LONDON • SYDNEY

Franklin Watts
First published in Great Britain in 2016 by
The Watts Publishing Group

Series editor: Amy Pimperton
Series designer: Jeni Child
Crafts: Rita Storey
Craft photography: Tudor Photography
Picture researcher: Diana Morris

Picture credits:
aroundworld/Shutterstock: 26-27 bg. Sinsia Botas/Shutterstock: 12c. Simon
Burchell/CC Wikimedia : 15t. daderot/CC Wikimedia : 11b. David Davis/
Dreamstime: 6b. De Agostini/Getty Images: 20c. De Agostini/Superstock: 16t.
Tamsin Dove/Shutterstock: 28b. Elegor/Shutterstock: 22-23 bg. Oscar Espinoza/
Shutterstock: 7t. Edouardo Estellez/Shutterstock: 11t. Werner Forman Archive:
6t, 10t, 12bl, 24t, 26b. Jan-Dirk Hansen/Shutterstock: 12tl. holbox/Shutterstock:
front cover. Jiang Hongyan/Shutterstock: 24b. Hugoht/Dreamstime: 4b, 30b.
jack photo/Shutterstock: 10-11 bg. Bernd Juergens/Shutterstock: 18c. Vladimir
Korostyshevskiy/Dreamstime: 26t, 32b. Patryk Kosmider/Dreamstime: 23b. Patryk
Kosmider/Shutterstock: 8b. Kravka/Dreamstime: 14t. Larry Larsen/Alamy: 16b.
Anne Lewis/Alamy: 14b. lightpoet/Shutterstock: 12tcl. Linear77/CC Wikimedia:
5t, 27cl. Lowe Art Museum, University of Miami/Bridgeman Art Library: 16c.
Raymond Pauly/Dreamstime: 12tc. Alexander Briel Perez/Dreamstime: 4t.
Pierdelune/Shutterstock: 27cr. Ondrej Prosicky/Dreamstime: 8t. Leon Rafael/
Shutterstock: 14-15bg. RAYPhotographer/Shutterstock: 18-19 bg. Tracy
Starr/Shutterstock: 4-5 bg. Successo Images/Shutterstock: 12tr. Tristan Tan/
Shutterstock: 10b. The Art Archive/Alamy: 19tr, 20t. Timin/Shutterstock: 12cl.
Paulo Vileia/Shutterstock: 12cr. Michal Wal/CC Wikimedia: 22c. Dongfan Wang/
Dreamstime: 1. CC Wikimedia : 28c. witoon214/Shutterstock: 12ccl. Wmpearl/
CC Wikimedia : 19tl. World History Archive/Alamy: 7b, 23t. Boris Yetshev/
Shutterstock: 28t.

HB ISBN: 978 1 4451 5048 2
PB ISBN: 978 1 4451 5049 9

Printed in China.

Franklin Watts
An imprint of
Hachette Children's Group
Part of The Watts Publishing Group
Carmelite House
50 Victoria Embankment
London EC4Y 0DZ

An Hachette UK company
www.hachette.co.uk

www.franklinwatts.co.uk

CONTENTS

Words in **bold** can be found in the glossary on page 30.

Some of the projects in this book require a craft knife, scissors, paint, glue, a needle, a hot glue gun and boiling water. We would recommend that children are supervised by an adult when using these things.

ALL ABOUT THE MAYA

The ancient Maya people first lived in Central America and southern Mexico over 2,300 years ago, which was around the same time as the Iron Age in Britain. Today, descendants of the Maya live in parts of the Yucatán region of Mexico.

City-states

The Maya cleared rainforests to grow crops and build great stone cities. Each city-state was a small kingdom – with its own ruler – but all Maya people shared the same skills, language and religion. At the centre of each city-state was a **sacred** city. The largest had hundreds of stone buildings, including grand temple-pyramids and palaces, libraries, hospitals, schools and ball courts.

Over 2 million Maya lived in 60 city-states scattered across the countries today known as Mexico, Guatemala, Belize and Honduras.

The ancient Maya civilisation was at the height of its power between 250 **BCE** and **CE** 900. This period of Maya history is known as the Classic period.

The ruins of a palace (far right) and temples (far left and centre, back) are all that remains of this small city-state in southern Mexico.

The Dresden Codex is one of the only surviving Maya codices. This is just one small section. The entire codex is over 3.5 metres long.

Maya skills

The Maya were skilled artists, architects, **engineers**, sculptors, weavers and potters. They developed their own form of writing and practised mathematics and **astronomy**. They wrote books, called codices, on paper they made from fig tree bark. Most were lost or destroyed when the Spanish **conquerors** arrived in the 1500s, but four Maya codices still survive today. Among Maya discoveries and inventions are: chocolate, which they made from **cacao** beans into a bitter, frothy drink; basketball and herbal medicine.

Quick FACTS

- the Maya lived in Central America and Mexico
- the Classic period was between 250 BCE and CE 900
- they lived in city-states ruled by kings
- they built great stone pyramids and grand buildings
- the Maya wrote books called codices

QUIZ TIME!

What did the Maya add to chocolate drinks?

a. herbs   **b. alcohol**   **c. chilli peppers**

Answer on page 32.

CITIES AND PEOPLE

The ruler of each city-state was the head of government and religion. Rulers raised taxes, made laws and led warriors into battle.

Maya peoples

Below the royal family came nobles and priests, then **merchants**, craftsmen, servants, and peasants who mostly worked on the land. The lowest social class were slaves. Maya women played an important role in society. They ran homes and raised children, prepared food and produced all the textiles and clothing. They worked as farmers, growing crops and raising herds of deer for venison. Some became priestesses and rulers.

This carving is of Yax-Pac. He was the last in a line of 16 kings of the Maya city-state of Copán.

The Maya word for pyramid was the same as the word for mountain. Some Maya pyramids were over 60 m high.

Sacred cities

The Maya used sharp flint stones to shape great blocks of limestone and sandstone for building. Within city walls, buildings were raised on mounds or stepped platforms, and set around courtyards or **plazas**. Walls were decorated with murals and carved stone

Stelae

Tall, carved stone markers, called stelae, stood around the plazas. These were carved with writing and images recording important events and victories in war, or showed scenes from Maya **myths**. The Maya also constructed bridges, **reservoirs**, systems for running water, and stone steam baths that were seen as a way to **purify** body and soul.

Stelae, like this one, were carved to praise rulers.

HAVE A GO
Design your own stela, using words and images to remember an important place, person or event in your life.

panels. Standing high above everything were great stone pyramids with steps leading to a temple used for religious ceremonies and **rituals**. The higher social classes lived in cities. Ordinary Maya lived in the surrounding countryside in simple thatched huts.

Bright colours

The Maya wore colourful clothing and both men and women decorated their bodies with paint, jewellery and tattoos. Ear flares were discs or squares of pottery, gold or precious stone that stretched the ear lobe. Clothing was closely linked to social rank, with rulers and nobles wearing the finest fabrics.

Jade was precious to the Maya. Only a ruler or a noble would have worn valuable jewellery like this jade pendant.

Quick *FACTS*

- the ruler of a city-state was the head of government and religion
- Maya belonged to different social classes
- they cut and carved huge blocks of stone by hand for building

? How did the Maya use feathers? Turn the page to find out.

Prized feathers

The Maya trapped birds for their feathers, which were used to decorate clothes, headdresses, fans, jewellery and weapons. The most prized were the bright-green tail feathers of the quetzal, which could measure up to a metre long. The quetzal was believed to represent wealth and freedom, and so its feathers were worn only by rulers and nobles.

The quetzal lives in **tropical** rainforests in Central and South America.

QUIZ TIME!

In Guatemala, what has the quetzal given its name to?

a. **money**
b. **a spicy drink**
c. **a feathered hat**

Answer on page 32.

Body art

Maya tattooed and painted their bodies and filed their teeth into points or T-shapes. Rulers and nobles had holes drilled into their front teeth, which were then filled with precious stones, such as jade and **obsidian**. When a baby was born, its head was squeezed between two wooden boards for a few days to flatten the shape of the skull. Crossed eyes were admired and parents encouraged them by hanging beads made from tree gum from the middle of a child's forehead.

This man is wearing a copy of a Maya feather headdress and body paint.

8

Make this

Fans decorated with colourful tropical birds' feathers were a symbol of status for rulers and nobles, and were carried by their **ambassadors** and messengers. Use craft feathers to make a Maya-style fan.

These brightly coloured fans would have looked very impressive to ordinary Maya people and to outsiders. They would also have been useful to help nobles keep cool in the hot, tropical rainforests of Central America.

1 Paint a small wooden spoon with gold paint on both sides. Leave to dry.

! Ask permission before you use the wooden spoon.

2 Cut out the shapes shown from stiff gold card. (Make the big circle large enough to cover the back of the spoon.) If you use plain card, paint the shapes gold and leave to dry.

3 Use a hot glue gun to glue five coloured craft sticks to the scooped side of the wooden spoon. Glue one of the curved card shapes to the ends of the craft sticks.

! Ask an adult to use the hot glue gun.

4 Glue feathers to the curved card shape. Glue the second curved shape on the ends of the feathers to hold them in place. Glue the large circle to the back of the spoon and the small circle to the front.

WORK AND TRADE

The Maya were skilled in many crafts, and craft objects and raw materials were traded between the city-states.

Travelling traders

Merchants did not use wheeled carts or animals to travel, instead they travelled mostly on foot between city-states, carrying goods in baskets. Some items were transported by sea in huge canoes made from hollowed-out tree trunks.

The Maya traded everyday goods, such as salt, food, clothes, stone tools and plain pottery. They also traded valuable items including gold, jade, decorated pottery and ritual objects. Cacao beans were so valuable they were used as a form of currency (money) or given as gifts.

This painted Maya pottery cup shows a servant (left) presenting a noble with various goods.

This cacao pod has been split open to reveal the brown cacao beans inside.

HAVE A GO
The Maya carried baskets on their head or on their back, held by straps around the forehead. Try walking with a flat bag or basket on your head to see if you can balance it.

Art and crafts

Craftsmen made stone and wood tools to farm, hunt and build. Pottery and tools were made in homes and community workshops. Sculptors carved stone panels. Painters painted murals on buildings and inside caves, and decorated sculptures, pottery and books. They used plant and **mineral pigments** including Maya blue, which was made using indigo from plant leaves mixed with a type of clay and then fired. Temples were painted red and the mineral mica was sometimes added to make them glitter under the sun's rays.

Mica gets its name from the Latin words *mica* ('crumb') and *micare* ('to shine').

Maya textiles

Maya women were skilled at spinning, dyeing and weaving. They made clothing and fine textiles including tapestries that may have been traded or given as gifts to rulers. They spun cotton by hand using clay **spindle whorls** and wove geometric, floral and animal patterns on portable **looms**. Many of the patterns carried a meaning, each of which would have been understood by the Maya. Every Maya community had its own unique textile patterns and colours.

This modern copy of Maya clothing shows the types of patterns and colours used by the Maya.

Quick FACTS

- merchants travelled on foot and by canoe
- they used cacao beans as currency
- Maya women made textiles and clothing
- craftsmen used stone and wood tools, and plant and mineral pigments were used for decoration

? What kinds of animals did the Maya keep? Turn the page to find out.

Pinto beans

Bees

Cassava

Sweet potato

Turkey

Maize (corn)

Chilli pepper

Papaya

Farming and hunting

Maya farmers cut down rainforest trees and drained wet areas to create areas where they could grow crops. The main crops were maize (corn), beans, squash, peppers, sweet potatoes and **cassava**. They cut terraces into steep hillsides and dug canals to water their crops. They also fished and hunted animals, such as turkeys, deer and wild pigs. They kept bees for honey and gathered fruits, such as papaya and watermelon.

Maya nobles used cups like this for drinking hot chocolate.

Meals and medicine

Maize was the **staple** food, eaten at every meal. It was ground into flour to make bread, pancakes, and dumplings that were filled with meat or vegetables. An alcoholic drink called *blache* was made from honey mixed with the bark of the blache tree. The beans from wild cacao trees were ground or roasted to make a frothy chocolate drink. It was a luxury enjoyed by rulers and nobles. It was also a medicine and was used in ritual ceremonies.

HAVE A GO
Melt 25 g of (unsweetened) baking chocolate with a little boiling water. Add a cup of boiling water, sprinkle with a dash of chilli powder or cinnamon then whisk until frothy.

! Ask an adult to pour on the boiling water and be careful with the chilli.

Make this

Nobles drank chocolate from clay cups, which were decorated with their name and images. Servants poured the chocolate from one cup to another to make it frothy.

Cacao is actually quite bitter – most of the chocolate we buy today is sweetened with sugar. Experts think the word chocolate comes from the Maya word *xocolatl*, which means 'bitter water'.

You can't drink from this chocolate cup as the water will make your cup soggy, but it would look great in a Maya-themed display. You could try painting a real, plain mug, with a Maya-style design to drink hot chocolate like a Maya noble! Make sure you ask permission before you paint on a mug.

1 Cut a strip of paper that will fit around a small crisp tube. Draw a Maya-inspired design, or create a design using your own name and face.

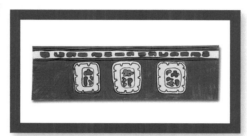

2 Paint most of it with terracotta-coloured paint to look like pottery. When it is dry, draw around the design outlines with a black felt-tip pen.

3 Paint the inside of the tube with gold paint. Leave to dry.

4 Wrap the strip tightly around the crisp tube. Tape the join closed with sticky tape. Use more tape on the bottom to keep the strip in place.

SPORT AND ENTERTAINMENT

The Maya enjoyed all kinds of sports and entertainment. They had outdoor stone theatres for watching plays and ball courts for competitive ball games.

Pok-A-Tok

Teams of seven competed against each other in the brutal game of Pok-A-Tok, using a solid rubber ball that could be as big as a basketball. They played on stone courts that had sloping walls painted with murals showing scenes from Maya battles or myths.

The courts had flat stone markers down the middle, and stone goal rings around the top of the walls. Players had to keep the ball in play by bouncing it from the hips, elbows and chest, without touching it with their hands or feet. They wore protective padding made from leather, and face masks.

The stone goal rings could be as high as 6 m from the ground.

These Pok-A-Tok **re-enactors** show off their skills in Yucatán, Mexico. The player in the middle has played the ball using his hip.

Victory and defeat

Games were an important part of festivals in Maya cities. Rulers and priests attended, sacred songs were sung and ceremonies held as the games were played in honour of the gods. The winning Pok-A-Tok team became heroes, but the losers could face dishonour and even death. Captives taken in war were sometimes forced to play, and if they lost they were killed as **sacrifices** to the gods. Some experts think that even the winning captain may have been offered as a worthy sacrifice!

El Tajín in Mexico was one of the largest Maya cities. It had more than 20 ball courts! This carving at its south ball court shows the sacrifice of a Pok-A-Tok player.

Board games

The Maya enjoyed gambling and played games of chance. The game of *patolli* was played on a mat, a board or on a grid scratched into the ground. Two or more players could compete. The aim was to be first to move a set of pebbles from one end of the board to the other, using five dried beans as dice.

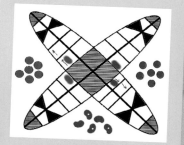

A patolli board is cross-shaped and is usually played with red and blue pebbles.

QUIZ TIME!

What did a Pok-A-Tok ball represent?

a. **the world**
b. **an enemy**
c. **the Sun**

Answer on page 32.

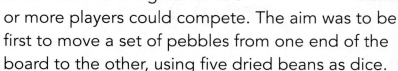

HAVE A GO
See how long you can keep a tennis ball or football in play using your hips, knees or elbows and without touching it with your hands or feet! It's harder than it sounds!

? What else were stone arenas used for? Turn the page to find out.

Music and entertainment

Rulers and nobles employed entertainers, such as singers, musicians and dancers. Plays were performed in outdoor stone theatres, which were also used for political meetings. Music played an important part in communicating with gods, **ancestors** and spirits. Music was also used in warfare to inspire troops, celebrate victory and to scare enemies in battle. It was played during important ceremonies, such as funerals.

This painting of a procession of musicians is a reconstruction of a wall painting in the Maya city of Bonampak.

Musical instruments

Long, curved trumpets were made from wood, clay or **gourds**. Gourds and turtle shells were also used to make rattles. Conch shells were pierced to make a kind of trumpet, and whistles and flutes were made from clay or bone, often in the shape of figures or animals. Drums made from animal skins and turtle shells were played using deer hooves or antlers. They ranged from huge, vertical wooden drums to small hand drums that fitted under the arm, so that the musicians could hold them while shaking rattles and bells.

This flute has been made in the shape of a double-headed jaguar.

Maya dancers and musicians also wore bells around their ankles.

Quick FACTS

- the Maya built theatres and ball courts
- they enjoyed music, dance and theatre
- music was important in war, religion and festivities
- they played trumpets, drums, flutes, whistles, rattles and bells

Make this

Bells were worn on belts and ankle cuffs or shaken on sticks by Maya dancers. The sound they made as the dancers performed would have been perfectly in time with their steps.

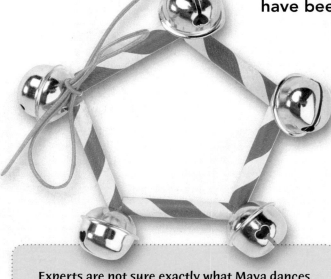

Experts are not sure exactly what Maya dances were like, but they think they probably copied movements of animals, such as jaguars and snakes, in some dances. Try making up a dance that uses animal-like movements. To make your dance extra noisy, you could make lots of ankle bells and stack them up on each ankle.

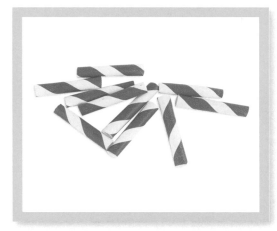

1 Cut straight, plastic drinking straws into lengths about 2.5 cm long. You'll need about five or six lengths for each one.

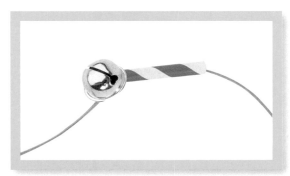

2 Cut a piece of thin elastic that is long enough to go twice around your ankle. Thread alternate bells and straws along the elastic until it fits around your ankle.

3 Tie the elastic in a knot and then in a bow as shown. (You may need to use a double knot.) Trim the ends. Stretch the elastic to slip it over your foot and onto your ankle.

WARFARE

The Maya fought wars over land, raw materials and trade routes, taking prisoners to use as slaves or sacrifices.

Maya cities were heavily defended with stone walls up to 3.5 m tall.

Attack and defence

Raids on enemy cities and land were often planned according to movements of planets or stars, which were thought to bring luck and victory. The losers had to pay a **tribute** to the victors, often in gold or silver, or prisoners who were marched back to conquering cities. Prisoners' clothes and jewellery were taken and they were tied and made to kneel before the ruler. Some had to take part in ball games that could end in death (see p. 15). Others were forced to be slaves.

Sometimes a ruler had to fight off attacks from rivals from within a city, who were trying to seize power. City-states also fought each other for power and larger cities sometimes took control of their smaller neighbours.

Fierce warriors

Warriors wore padded armour made from leather or cotton padded with rock salt. They carried protective shields, and weapons made of wood and shells. Faces and bodies were painted black and red, and they wore jaguar skins and helmets or headdresses. Shields and helmets were decorated with images of jaguars and other fierce animals, as warriors believed it gave them strength. As they attacked, warriors yelled, hissed, banged drums, blew horns and shook rattles to make themselves seem fierce and to scare the enemy.

This warrior statue carries a round shield and wears an elaborate headdress.

HAVE A GO
See how the Maya made body armour. Stitch or glue two squares of cotton together leaving one side open. Pack tightly with rock salt or coarse sea salt then stitch or glue the open side. How easy is it to pierce with a stick or needle?

! Ask permission before you do this and ask an adult to supervise you with the needle.

? What weapons did Maya warriors use for hand-to-hand combat? Turn the page to find out.

Weapons

When they were attacking from a distance, warriors used bows and arrows, slings and throwing spears. Fighting hand-to-hand, they used clubs, axes, spears and knives. Clubs and axes were made from wood and had sharp blades made from flint or obsidian, a hard volcanic rock.

This highly decorated shield may or may not have been used in battle. It is covered with incredible patterns in turquoise mosaic.

Round shields and throwing spears can be seen in this Maya battle scene.

QUIZ TIME!

How were gourds used as a weapon?

a. they were filled with poison

b they were filled with hornets and wasps

c. they were filled with rocks

Answer on page 32.

Quick *FACTS*

- cities fought each other for land and trade routes
- cities had defensive stone walls to protect them against attack
- the losing side had to pay a tribute
- Maya warriors used a variety of weapons for attack and defence

Make this

Warriors carried square or round shields. Some were woven mat shields that folded flat. Others were made from deerskin that was stretched over a wooden frame.

Jaguars are big cats that are native to the rainforests of Central and South America. The jaguar was a very sacred animal to the Maya and they worshipped several jaguar gods. Research jaguars on the Internet to find out why the Maya linked jaguars as gods of the underworld and of the night, and why jaguars were associated with warfare.

1 Use a craft knife to cut a circle of foam board about 50 cm in diameter. Paint it black. Leave to dry.

! Ask an adult to use the craft knife.

2 Draw around the foam board on a piece of yellow paper. Draw a jaguar head with a black felt-tip pen. Cut it out.

3 Glue the jaguar head to the foam board, lining up the curves along the edge.

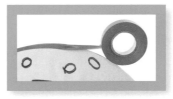

4 Tape all around the edge with green plastic tape.

5 Cut two strips of card. Tape them to the back of the shield with the green tape as shown. The two loops should be just wide enough to fit your arm through.

RELIGION AND MEDICINE

The Maya worshipped many gods through prayer, rituals and sacrifices. They believed that praying to the gods would bring them success, wealth and happiness.

The tongue was a common body part used in bloodletting. Here Lady Xoc (a Maya queen) draws a thorny rope through her tongue!

Gods, ancestors and spirits

They believed that gods, ancestors and spirits could hurt or help them, so they had to keep them happy with offerings. If they did not, they believed the gods punished them with disasters, such as **drought**, **plague** or even **chaos** in the universe. They believed that only human blood and hearts could satisfy the gods, so they offered them through rituals of **bloodletting** and sacrifice.

The highest of the gods was Itzamna, the creator god of fire and hearth. There were many other nature gods, such as the gods of the Sun, Moon, rain and lightning, maize and cacao.

Priests and sacrifices

Priests performed human sacrifices on raised platforms, sometimes in temples on pyramids. They used a knife to cut out the victim's heart, which was burned as an offering. Victims' bodies were placed in caves or holes in the ground, which were seen as passages to the underworld. Many sacrificial victims were slaves, but rulers and nobles also went through ritual bloodletting. Nobles' flesh was stabbed with plant or fish spines, and strings of thorns were pulled through their tongues. Their blood was collected on paper or cloth and then burned as an offering.

This Maya statue of a priest is holding a ritual knife in his right hand.

Healers and medicine

Healers or **medicine men** used plants to make herbal medicines. They were skilled at stitching wounds using human hair, repairing bone breaks and filling teeth or making false teeth from jade and turquoise. They used plant drugs to go into a **trance** state, which they thought would allow them to communicate with the gods and enter the spirit world.

A re-enactor demonstrating a trance-like state performs in a ceremony.

HAVE A GO
The Maya understood the healing powers of cacao. Use the Internet to research five ways chocolate is good for you.

? Where did the Maya believe the dead went? Turn the page to find out.

Burial and afterlife

The Maya believed that after they died, their souls must journey through the underworld – a dangerous place full of demons – before they could join the god of maize in heaven. Only those who had died while giving birth or through sacrifice would go straight to heaven. Priests held ceremonies to keep the demons happy so they did not harm the living. Poor people buried their relatives under the floors of their houses so their ancestors would be close by. Rulers and nobles

This jade funerary mask was placed over King Pakal the Great's face. He was buried in a tomb in the Temple of Inscriptions in the Maya city of Palenque.

were buried in tombs, some in burial chambers inside pyramids. They were buried with treasures including **funerary** masks, figures of servants and entertainers, books, jade masks, necklaces and earrings.

QUIZ TIME!

How did the Maya imagine the underworld?

a. hot and fiery   **b. watery**   **c. thickly forested**

Answer on page 32.

Maize

This crop was highly important to the Maya and it was seen as a symbol of rebirth. During burial rituals, the dead had maize placed in their mouth as the Maya believed they would need food on their journey to the underworld.

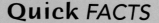

Quick FACTS

- the Maya worshipped many gods, ancestors and spirits
- priests sacrificed victims as offerings to the gods
- nobles were buried with jade and other precious objects
- the Maya believed the dead went to an underworld

Make this

The Maya wore decorative masks for important events, in battle and after burial. The most precious were funerary masks made from jade. They were thought to protect the dead as they entered the underworld.

Use your funerary mask as part of a display on Maya culture. Funerary masks can be found in many cultures all over the world, including the ancient Egyptians. Do some research to find out about funerary masks from other cultures. What similarities and differences can you find?

1 Blow up a balloon and cover half of it with several layers of papier-mâché. Leave to dry.

2 Bend a small piece of card as shown. Use masking tape to attach it to the balloon. This is your mask's nose.

3 Cover the nose with more layers of papier-mâché. When it is dry, paint it white, pop the balloon and then trim the edges of the mask.

4 Glue pieces of green paper to cover the mask. Draw two eye shapes and a mouth shape on white paper with black and red felt-tip pens. Cut them out and stick them on.

WRITING AND ASTRONOMY

The Maya were an advanced civilisation for the time and had their own systems of writing, mathematics and astronomy.

The Maya joined glyphs together to spell out words and sentences. These glyphs have been carved into stone.

Scribes and books

The Maya used a form of picture writing, based on around 800 glyphs. A glyph is a symbol that stands for words or sounds. Writing was thought of as a sacred gift from the gods.

Trained **scribes** kept records of property and estates, and recorded family histories. Maya writing was carved onto stone, bone and wood or painted onto plaster, paper and pottery. It records religious rituals, victories in war and important dates and events.

Codex

The bark paper used for codices (see p. 5) was whitened with lime, then folded and bound with deerskin, jaguar skin or wood. Some were **almanacs** that recorded the movements of the planets and **solar eclipses**. Books were often placed with other treasures in tombs.

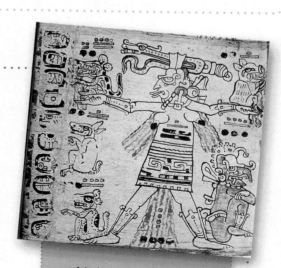

This is a page from the Madrid Codex. It shows rainfall and a goddess of the Moon.

Counting numbers

The Maya recorded numbers using three main signs: a dot (one), bar (five) and a shell (zero). Numbers up to twenty were written using combinations of these signs. Counting accurately was important for trading goods, calculating dates, and predicting solar eclipses and other important events.

Bars, dots and shells can be seen in these painted Maya numbers.

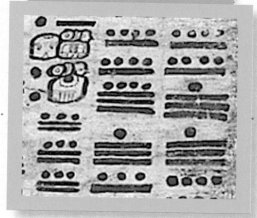

Astronomy

Astronomers kept tables that plotted the position of the Sun, Moon, stars and planets. These were used by priests to advise rulers of the right time to sow and harvest, when to go to war and when to hold ceremonial events. Battles were often fought at times when the planet Venus was rising in the sky.

Experts think this round building was a Maya observatory – a place where the Maya would observe the stars, Sun and planets.

HAVE A GO
Try writing the numbers 1–19 using the Maya system of recording numbers. Wherever you have a combination of dots and lines, the dots should be above the lines. Counting over 20 is a bit trickier. Can you find out how to write the number 22?

QUIZ TIME!
What did the Maya see in the moon?

a. a rabbit   b. a man   c. a snake

Answer on page 32.

? How accurate were Maya calendars?
Turn the page to find out.

Maya calendars

The Maya used mathematics and astronomy to develop accurate calendars. One, based on observation of the Sun's position in the sky, had a 365-day year. A 260-day sacred calendar was used to decide which were lucky or unlucky days to plan important events or name children. The Maya believed that the universe went through cycles of destruction and re-creation. They recorded these long periods in a third calendar called the Long Count.

This is a famous Aztec calendar called the Sun Stone. The Aztecs were a later civilisation in Mexico. Maya calendars would have looked almost exactly the same as this one.

Francisco Hernández de Córdoba was a Spanish conqueror who encountered the Maya in 1517.

What happened?

By about 1000 CE the Maya civilisation was in decline. Nobody really knows why, though it may have been because of foreign invasions, disease, drought or war. When Spanish conquerors arrived from Europe 500 years later, they brought new diseases that killed more than half the remaining Maya population. Today around 6 million descendants of the ancient Maya live in Mexico and Central America.

Quick FACTS

- the Maya developed their own form of writing
- they devised methods for recording and calculating numbers
- Maya astronomers plotted the positions of stars and planets

These traditional Maya textiles are on display in a market in Guatemala.

Make this

Many Maya glyphs were carved into stone. This would have been a skilled and tough job as the Maya only had stone tools to chip away the rock and carve fine details. Make your own Maya-style glyph from air-dry clay.

Use the Internet to look for real Maya glyphs to copy or make up more of your own. Include animals, the Moon or Sun, people and plants. Can you use the glyphs to make up a story?

1 Take a ball of air-dry clay and roll it until it is about 1 cm thick. Use a blunt kitchen knife to cut a square base, roughly 2.5 cm x 2.5 cm.

2 Roll and flatten blobs of clay into shapes, such as circles and more squares. Stick them to the base using water.

3 Use a cocktail stick to scratch patterns and make dots in the clay pieces. Leave your glyph to completely air dry.

4 Paint the glyph using terracotta paint so it looks like sandstone.

GLOSSARY

almanac important dates and information for the year ahead

ambassador an important person who visits a place instead of a ruler or noble

ancestors dead relatives

astronomy the study of space, stars and planets

BCE dates before the year 1. The letters stand for Before Common Era

bloodletting a ritual where blood is spilled deliberately

cacao the beans or seeds of the cacao tree

cassava a type of tree root

CE dates after the year 1. The letters stand for Common Era

chaos disorder or confusion

conqueror a person who takes over a place or a country, usually by force

drought a long period with little or no rain

engineer someone who designs and builds buildings or machines

funerary to do with burials or funerals

gourd a type of large, hard-shelled fruit

government a group of people who govern a country and make laws

Iron Age the period of history after the Bronze Age, when people first used the metal, iron

jade a stone that contains the mineral, jadeite

loom a machine for weaving cloth

medicine men healers thought to have magic powers to cure diseases

merchant a trader

mineral a natural substance that is formed of crystals

myths traditional stories or legends

obsidian a hard, dark, glass-like volcanic rock

pigments colours that come from natural materials

plague a contagious disease that spreads quickly and kills people

plazas city squares

purify to clean

re-enactor someone who recreates past events

reservoir a large lake used as a water supply

ritual actions performed in a certain order at a ceremony

sacred connected to gods or religion

sacrifice something offered to the gods

scribes writers or clerks

solar eclipse when the Moon passes between the Sun and Earth, blocking the Sun's light

spindle whorls clay discs that were attached to spindles to make them spin thread faster

staple basic or everyday

taxes a payment to a state or ruler

trance a dream-like state

tribute a forced payment

tropical the hot, humid places on Earth that lie on either side of the Equator

BOOKS

Explore!: Mayan Civilisations by Izzi Howell (Wayland)

Great Civilisations: The Maya by Tracey Kelly (Franklin Watts)

The History Detective Investigates: Mayan Civilisation by Clare Hibbert (Wayland)

History in Infographics: The Mayans by Jon Richards (Wayland)

The Story of Chocolate by Alex Woolf (Wayland)

Technology in the Ancient World: The Maya and other American Civilisations by Charlie Samuels (Franklin Watts)

PLACES TO VISIT

There are some Maya objects that are in museum collections in the UK, notably at the British Museum in London: www.britishmuseum.org/

You can visit Maya ruins at many ancient sites including:
Caracol in Belize: www.mayan-ruins.org/caracol/
Copán in Honduras: http://whc.unesco.org/en/list/129
Tikal in Guatemala: http://whc.unesco.org/en/list/64
Chichen Itza in Mexico: www.chichenitza.com/

WEBSITES

Lots of information about Maya religion, sport, music and dance:
http://www.mayas.mrdon

All about the Maya, including a video showing their great achievements and inventions:
http://www.history.com/topics/maya

Information about the people, culture and gods, with news on recent discoveries by archaeologists at Maya sites.
http://www.mayankids.com

NOTE TO PARENTS AND TEACHERS:

Every effort has been made by the Publishers to ensure that these websites are suitable for children, that they are of the highest educational value, and that they contain no inappropriate or offensive material. However, because of the nature of the Internet, it is impossible to guarantee that the contents of these sites will not be altered. We strongly advise that Internet access is supervised by a responsible adult.

QUIZ ANSWERS

Page 5. c – chilli peppers.
Page 8. a – money. The quetzal is the official currency of Guatemala and the quetzal bird also appears on Guatemala's flag.
Page 15. c – the Sun. The stone scoring rings were also said to represent sunrise and sunset.
Page 20. b – they were filled with hornets and wasps!
Page 24. b – watery.
Page 27. c – a rabbit. The Maya thought the pattern of the markings on the surface of the Moon as seen from Earth are in the shape of a rabbit. Next time there is a full moon, have a look for yourself. Can you see a rabbit shape?

* Page 27: the Maya would have written the number 22 as: